A. AUBREY BODINE *Baltimore Pictorialist, 1906–1970*

PORTRAIT OF A. AUBREY BODINE, BY HOLMES METTES, 1927

A. AUBREY BODINE
Baltimore Pictorialist, 1906–1970

by KATHLEEN M. H. EWING   *with a Remembrance by HAROLD A. WILLIAMS*

THE JOHNS HOPKINS UNIVERSITY PRESS
Baltimore and London

© 1985 The Johns Hopkins University Press
All rights reserved
Printed in the United States of America

*Copyright of all photographs belongs to the estate of
A. Aubrey Bodine.*

The Johns Hopkins University Press
701 West 40th Street
Baltimore, Maryland 21211
The Johns Hopkins Press Ltd., London

LIBRARY OF CONGRESS
CATALOGING-IN-PUBLICATION DATA
Ewing, Kathleen.
  A. Aubrey Bodine, Baltimore pictorialist,
1906–1970.
  Bibliography: p.
  1. Photography, Artistic.   2. Bodine, A. Aubrey,
1906–1970.   I. Bodine, A. Aubrey, 1906–1970.
II. Title.
TR653.E95   1985   779'.092'4   85-45042
ISBN 0-8018-3151-2 (alk. paper)

*The paper in this book is acid-free and meets the
guidelines for permanence and durability of the Committee
on Production Guidelines for Book Longevity of the Council
on Library Resources.*

CONTENTS

ACKNOWLEDGMENTS

I first saw an exhibition of A. Aubrey Bodine's photographs in a New York gallery in 1977. Many of the images were from his early work, in the 1930s, and I was surprised that they did not conform to my preconception of Bodine as a regional photographer. I was just then beginning to appreciate the beauty and diversity of American pictorialism. In 1979, I was privileged to meet Aubrey Bodine's widow, Nancy, and his daughter, Jennifer, and I began working directly with the vast collection of photographs left in their care. Unfortunately, I never met Aubrey Bodine. I do believe, however, that we would have shared an interest in photographic romanticism and a devotion to the medium.

There are many persons whose support and guidance have made this book possible, too many to mention individually. A few deserve special recognition. The cooperation of the staff of the *Baltimore Sun* has been particularly important, as access to the *Sun* archives gave me a significant source of information. The staff of the Johns Hopkins University Press, especially the regional editor, Nancy Essig, is to be commended for their patience in seeing me through my first book. Steve Szabo's assistance in research and image selection, as well as his photographic insight, was invaluable. Finally, this book could not have been accomplished without Nancy Bodine. I sincerely believe that she was the loving stabilizing influence in Aubrey Bodine's life and in many ways enabled him to produce these exceptional photographs that have enriched generations of admirers.

A. AUBREY BODINE *Baltimore Pictorialist, 1906–1970*

SYMPHONY IN REFLECTIONS, 1925

A. AUBREY BODINE   *The Man and the Colleague*

by Harold A. Williams

To say that A. Aubrey Bodine was a photographer for the *Baltimore Sunday Sun* for forty-three years, from 1927 to 1970, does not begin to convey what he did or the reputation and influence he achieved. His captivating portrayal of Maryland became the eye-catching showpiece of the Sunday package. In fact, many subscribers bought the paper solely because of his pictures. Before long his work became known beyond the reaches of the *Sun.* He exhibited across the country and around the world, in salons that attracted the best artistic photographers. By competing in that métier with newspaper pictures—a startling development—he became an innovator and a force among artistic photographers and he enlarged the dimensions of newspaper photography.

This is how it all began:

In the 1920s, thirties, early forties Bodine's pictures appeared in the sepia-colored photogravure section, known as the Brown Section, which also had syndicated shots of national and international events (these invariably included a dreadnought firing a salvo or a rider being thrown in a steeplechase). At first his pictures were of recurrent photogravure favorites—the Maryland Hunt Cup, graduation at the Naval Academy, duck hunting, and the big local news of that day, Queen Marie of Rumania visiting the city, Lindbergh speaking at the stadium in the rain. But gradually his own distinctive style evolved. On March 28, 1928, a large photograph entitled "Evening in the Harbor'" appeared. Made at dusk and showing the rigging of oyster boats

against a somber sky, it had a haunting quality that made it different from newspaper pictures. It carried the credit line "A. Aubrey Bodine" and was probably his first regular *Sun* credit. From then on, the Brown Section was graced with Bodine's pictorial photography portraying Maryland, from the mountains to the Atlantic, capturing its diversity and beauty, its moods, its people and their work.

After World War II, the photogravure section was replaced by the *Sun Magazine,* one of the first newspaper rotogravure magazines, and it became the showcase for Bodine's talent. Bodine caught the picturesque Bay watermen crabbing and oystering, farmers growing tobacco in the flat land of tidewater and shocking corn on the rolling ridges of the piedmont, mountain folk picking ginseng or searching out wells with divining rods. He captured Baltimore life from the serenity of Mount Vernon Place to the belching blast furnaces of Sparrows Point. The bustling harbor, the stretching Chesapeake Bay and its inviting estuaries were favorite hunting grounds. Many of his memorable pictures captured ships gliding into the harbor at dawn or dusk, skipjacks and bugeyes, along with graceful log canoes, their sails taut with wind, racing across sparkling waters. The *Magazine*'s most popular feature was the Maryland Gallery, a series of full-page scenes by Bodine. Intended to run for about a year, it became so popular that it appeared almost every week for years. These and other of his pictures were studied in schools, pasted in scrapbooks, and hung in crossroad garages. To a Marylander, the name *Bodine* conjured a vision of a beautiful picture, and a beautiful picture of Maryland was instantly associated with *Bodine.* The byline "A. Aubrey Bodine," with the possible exception of the byline "H. L. Mencken," became the best known in the history of the *Sun.*

I had worked as a *Sun Magazine* reporter with Bodine for two years, then as editor of the *Magazine,* and later as editor of the *Sunday Sun* for nearly twenty years, so I was familiar with many of the attributes that constituted his art. I was particularly impressed, though occasionally chagrined, by his proverbial patience (especially for a newspaper photographer) in waiting for the precise moment to capture the essence he sought. Two examples: He went to Federal Hill thirty or forty times before 6 A.M. to make a color shot of the Baltimore skyline and never took the camera from his car. He marked time during a cold April until he could photograph the Middletown Valley in its first filmy lace of spring. Just as he was about to make the picture the light failed. Without a word he put his camera and tripod in the car and drove the fifty miles back to Baltimore. He stoically waited for another April to get what he wanted.

He was not only patient in making his pictures—he spoke of making rather than taking them—but painstaking as well. Once asked how an assignment turned out, he replied, "Didn't open my camera. I'm having them dig a pit so I can get silhouettes from a new angle." Another time, noticing that we did not have a good picture of the Maryland Historical Society, I asked him to make one. This was in February. He immediately responded that he would make it in late April. I knew well enough not to hurry him. Knowing the area—he lived nearby—he had calculated when the early morning light would strike the building in its most enhancing way. He didn't have to be reminded of the assignment. The day before he planned to make the picture he had Nancy, his wife, ask the Police Department to put up No Parking signs on streets bordering the

building. He asked James Foster, director of the society, to have the doors open at 5 A.M. and the American and state flags flying from their third-floor poles. Since it seemed unreasonable to ask a staff member to appear at such an early hour, the aging Mr. Foster came down, got the flags raised, opened the doors, and picked litter off the sidewalks. Bodine arrived a few minutes before five o'clock and his picture was made by five. When it appeared in the Maryland Gallery it undoubtedly inspired amateurs to duplicate it. Their snaps, made on a Sunday afternoon stroll, didn't turn out as well, and they probably consoled themselves with a comment often heard, "Oh, well. Bodine has much better equipment than I do."

After hearing such excuses, I asked Bodine to buy a two-dollar box camera to photograph Baltimore. Using sunlight, shadow, and ingenuity, he turned in a stunning set of pictures. A row of commonplace buildings with jumbled roof lines and chimneys was somehow made to reflect the title he gave them, "Air Castles." Later, exhibited widely, it won many awards. To retain clouds in a shot of the Washington Monument, he used his sun glasses as a filter. He double exposed his last shot, as amateurs often do when they forget to turn the film. But he did it adroitly, and it became a study of reflecting patterns.

His favorite camera was a 5 × 7 Linhof view camera mounted on a tripod. Both looked as if they had been abandoned on a Civil War battlefield by Mathew Brady, one of the few photographers Bodine admired. The trunk of his car—its capacity was often a factor when he bought a car—contained, in addition to photographic equipment, a machete, a shovel, a child's white parasol, a bee smoker, and toilet paper. Machete and shovel were used to chop down or dig out anything, from brush to fence posts, that obstructed his camera angle; the parasol was raised when he needed a softer light; the toilet paper was wrapped around flash bulbs for a diffused light. On my first assignment as a reporter with him he tossed me the bee smoker after lighting its damp straw and ordered me to keep waving it beside the camera until he told me to stop. He didn't explain, and it wasn't until I saw the print that I realized how my wisps of smoke had helped create a mood.

Bodine was skillful in adding elements. For photographs made on a clear day he would select his own clouds. Only occasionally did sharp-eyed readers detect what he had done; one noticed billowing cumulus clouds filling the sky while narrow bands of cirrus were reflected in the Potomac River below. Most of Bodine's clouds were made in New England. He said he couldn't think of a better vacation than lying on his back on a hillside shooting clouds. His pictures were used to show the variety of Maryland scenery in a *Magazine* feature, "America the Beautiful." A meteorologist told Bodine he had never seen cloud formations more typical in Maryland. Bodine didn't let on that the cloud formations had been made in other states, but, a firm believer that most experts did not know what they were talking about, he often told that anecdote to illustrate his point.

He used other elements besides clouds: A photograph of an abandoned farmhouse had a large bird's nest spilling over the sides of the chimneytop. The scene had acceptable clouds, but, feeling it lacked a dramatic component, Bodine added a circling osprey. He photographed a sunbonneted old woman standing in the doorway of her crumbling house in Frederick. Then, back in his darkroom, to the uncurtained window he added, with great skill, an incongruous but sympathetic gift—a vase of flowers. (Later he wrote the mayor and the editor of the Frederick paper, prodding them to do something about the woman's wretched living conditions.)

Imagination also helped get him what he wanted. The house that stands on the site of the Johnson Tavern would not have made an appealing picture in daylight, so, in *Chesapeake Bay and Tidewater,* Bodine photographed it silhouetted by moonlight. That gave a feeling of mystery and intrigue, the right mood, because the old tavern had been the headquarters of Patty Cannon,

notorious murderer and kidnapper of free blacks. On another occasion, he picked a burly, crag-faced waterman to photograph at the tiller of his boat, garbed in a sou'wester hat and slicker. But he felt he needed something more to give the picture an added dimension, so he had the reporter get a bucket of cold water and stand behind the waterman. At Bodine's signal the reporter threw the water in the waterman's face. Bodine caught the startled expression and the water running in rivulets down the face and the slicker.

He seldom "bracketed" his shots as most photographers do, with varying exposures and angles. He relished showing off his "one-shot" confidence whenever he thought he could unnerve someone who had annoyed him by offering suggestions. At West Point, for example, he made just one picture of the academy superintendent. Aides and public relations nail-biters, hovering behind him, whispered nervously, "Don't you think you'd better shoot a couple more to be sure? "Nah," he replied loud enough for all to hear, "I just need one of him."

If he was not recognized when taking a picture on the street, onlookers would usually ask, "What paper is that going to be in?" Bodine would just point a finger to the sun. Some caught on.

Starting in the 1920s, but particularly in the forties and fifties, his newspaper pictures, enlarged and presented in one of eleven different processes, though often gold-toned, were exhibited in museums, art galleries, and photographic salons across the United States. He exhibited regularly in the Photographic Society of America competitions and was ranked as one of the top exhibitors for the number of prints accepted by judges. Unlike many competitors, who entered only past winners, Bodine attempted to average a new picture for each salon. Between 1943 and 1948 he twice finished first in national competition; once he was second and once third. He was named an Honorary Fellow of the society "for his talent, accomplishments and encouraging influence on photography as an art." Only twenty others had been given that honor, including Edward Steichen, Alfred Stieglitz, and Edward Weston.

In addition to uncounted medals, trophies, ribbons, and cash awards won in salon and other competitions, his "Oyster Dredgers" won first prize, a $5,000 savings bond, in a contest sponsored by *Popular Photography* which attracted 51,038 entries. The next year in the same contest, which drew 53,554 entries, his "Early Morning Charge" won second prize. He considered that unlikely feat among his major achievements. In the 1950s, when the *Encyclopaedia Britannica* cosponsored an annual competition with the National Press Photographers Association, he won twelve sets of the encyclopaedia, many sets of the junior encyclopaedia, and numerous dictionaries and atlases. *Life* printed his pictures for having won this astounding number, and he was soon besieged with hundreds of requests for a free set. He had given all but one away to friends and schools as soon as he won them. In his set the first reference he checked was the listing for Mathew Brady. Astonished and angered to find no mention, he bombarded the encyclopaedia editors with telegrams and letters until they finally included the Brady biography.

In the 1950s, needing new worlds to conquer, Bodine began exhibiting abroad, and his name became well known internationally, although the Soviet Union got it wrong. When he was awarded a gold medal by the Soviets—probably the first given to an American photographer—he learned about it from an admirer in the Soviet section of the National Security Agency. Reading *Pravda* she had noticed his name, but it was given as "Bodine Aubrey."

The popularity of his work led to the publication of a number of books by Bodine and Associates. The first was *My Maryland* in 1952; *Chesapeake Bay and Tidewater,* his most successful book, in 1954; *The Face of Maryland* in 1961; *The Face of Virginia* in 1963; and two guide books, *A Guide to Baltimore and Annapolis* in 1957 and *Baltimore Today* in 1969. *Bodine's Baltimore: Forty-six Years in the Life of a City,* was published posthumously in 1973. The first four books have had a number of printings and revisions, and all his titles have sold more than 110,000 copies.

In September 1943, H. L. Mencken wrote to Bodine that he was at work on a supplement to *The American Language* and was "trying to embellish it with a number of vocabularies of trade argots." He solicited Bodine's help in compiling a vocabulary used by newspaper photographers. Bodine replied almost a year later with twelve examples, including *soup* for developer, *fuzz ball* for a negative that is out of focus, and *lens louse* for "one who insists on getting in the picture, invariably spoiling the set up. For example, Joe Tipman. Visit his bar, next to Miller Brothers, and see the vast collection of pictures he has horned in on." In the second supplement Bodine is credited for his contributions.

After his death in 1970 I wrote the biography *Bodine, A Legend in His Time.* In talking to his wife, Nancy, his daughter, Jennifer, and his doctor at different times I was given much the same appraisal—they never really knew him. His doctor's words were, "I was terribly fond of him, but I never really understood the man. And I'm not sure anyone else did either." The *Sun* published a special magazine of his work after his death and in the text for it I wrote: "To his friends he was a free spirit, an uncommon man, an artist not only in ability but in temperament, and, in this age of conformity, one of the last truly rugged and colorful individualists. An associate described him as a man of cast-iron whims. Ralph Reppert [a reporter and one of Bodine's best friends] was convinced that if Bodine had fallen off of a boat and drowned his body would have floated upstream."

He had many pet hates: the Red Cross, potatoes baked in tinfoil jackets, editorial writers, race horses, antivivisectionists, Howard Johnson restaurants, long pencils, plastic, pie cut in more than four slices, liberals, Palmolive soap commercials, the National Safety Council, and wedding bands for men. When Jennifer was planning her marriage he warned her that he would disown her if she had a double-ring ceremony. Her engagement picture, which he gave to the Society Page editor for publication in the *Sunday Sun,* was a passport-size print made by another photographer.

While Bodine was a member of the Charcoal Club, founded in 1885 by artists and in its heyday conspicuous for its unconventional stunts and parties, the president would never table any matter of business, no matter how impractical or outrageous it might be, but would always say "Referred to the Bodine Committee." Now and then Bodine would astound the president and the members by taking an off-the-wall suggestion and developing it as a worthwhile idea. The challenge and the perversity appealed to him.

He was about 5 foot 10 but seemed taller, had sorrel-colored hair, a no-nonsense air, and a smile that was warmer and more frequent than one might expect. He seemed continually alert and never missed the slightest detail, whether he was assaying a potential scene or browsing in a country store. He had a flair for colorful expressions; as a friend put it, "Once he described something you never forgot it." He swore frequently and with fervor.

A fastidious dresser, though with a flair different from that of others, he wore bright-colored suits, custom-made shirts with distinctive stripes and white collars (this decades before they became stylish), white shoes in summer, and in fall and winter, a tattersall vest and homburg. His shoes were English, his coats by Burberry or tailor-made, his silk suits Italian, and his hats by Borsalino. He dressed well except for his roughest assignments or when he went to a doctor, which was often during his last years when his health had deteriorated. Because he didn't want "them" to think he was wealthy, he wore an old suit that Nancy called "the doctor's suit." He was always urging his friends to wear and have what he wore and had, be it Lotus shoes or a Chambers gas range. (He insisted I buy both.) To needle Bodine for his cracks about the way he dressed, Reppert

wrote in a magazine article about him that Bodine "dressed in the colorful good taste of a well-heeled Senator from one of the peckerwood states."

Bodine smoked corncob pipes all day long, but I don't recall ever seeing him smoke at home. In his introduction to *The Face of Maryland* he noted: "I am an inveterate corncob pipe smoker, and I use more matches than tobacco. When I am at Tulip Hill [a Georgian mansion on the West River in Anne Arundel County]—which I regard as a perfect house and exquisitely kept—I put my matches in my pocket and risk burning my coat rather than soil one of its ashtrays." In some pictures I've noticed his corncob pipe in an ashtray placed inconspicuously in the library of a tidewater mansion, on a porch railing of an antique shop, on a table in Mencken's home, or on a wharf piling. I asked him if he meant that as a "signature," as a pair of boots, placed in the foreground of a battlefield scene, was a Mathew Brady "signature." He shrugged and walked off without answering, but I'm convinced that it was. One other story: When he needed a new car he couldn't decide what make best suited his needs. At many lunches he talked about horsepower and raised questions about the gas consumption and trunk capacity of various makes. Finally, he picked a Ford Galaxie. "Why that?" he was asked. "The Ford Motor Car Company," he explained, "is the only one that makes an ashtray big enough for two corncob pipes."

He never spoke of his life before he became a *Sunday Sun* photographer other than to say that he had attended St. Paul's School. He was born in Baltimore July 21, 1906, into a family of modest means. His father supplemented his income by setting up penny gum and candy machines in drug and grocery stores. His mother, who painted landscapes and still lifes as a hobby, sold her diamond engagement ring so that Aubrey could attend St. Paul's. Checking payroll records near his fiftieth anniversary on the paper I was surprised to discover that he had started as a messenger in 1920, at the age of 14, for eight dollars a week. Though I knew him well as a colleague and friend, I had never heard him mention that. When I asked him about this he managed to sidle away without answering. He was a messenger four years before being promoted to commercial photographer in 1924, to take pictures of ice boxes, bedroom suites, and automobiles for advertisements. He did that until 1927, when he became a *Sunday Sun* photographer. In *Who's Who* and other biographies he gave his date of employment as 1924. His *Who's Who* sketch had five misleading major facts exaggerating his career. Some husbands might occasionally forget the date of their wedding anniversary; Bodine listed the wrong date for his.

He was surprisingly shy in many ways, but he was also that rare individual who said and did what he pleased, no matter the time or place. Photographing a Guilford mansion he pointedly asked the lady of the house, "Who talked you into buying *that* wallpaper?" It turned out that she was on the Women's Volunteer Board of the Keswick Home with Nancy, and that strained matters a bit for a time. A further complication arose when the lady met Aubrey's brother, Seeber, socially and mistook him for the photographer. "Why didn't you like my drawing-room wallpaper?" she asked him. Seeber, of course, didn't know what she was talking about, and the conversation went in circles until his fraternal identity was established.

Soon after she was married, Bodine's stepdaughter, Stuart, gave her first family party. Her mother-in-law, noted as a painstaking gourmet cook, especially for her Caesar's salad, prepared one for the party. At dinner Bodine tasted the salad, and, thinking it had been made by his stepdaughter, announced, "Stuart, you ought to give up housekeeping right now if you can't make a better salad than this." Though Nancy whispered that it was the creation of the mother-in-law, who looked as if she was ready to dump it in his lap, he made no effort to make amends. His opinion stood, family crisis or not.

At the Naval Academy, an admiral making

conversation wondered why the navy did not have better photographers. Bodine, without looking up from his camera, observed, "If you stupid bastards had enough sense to offer decent ratings to men who know their business you'd get photographers, not A&P clerks!" He was so conservative in his politics that he regarded John Birchers as flaming liberals. He had no use for the Kennedys—Joe, Rose, their children, their children's spouses and their families, and he particularly disliked Bobby.

The late Edward L. Bafford, a noted amateur Baltimore photographer who had known Bodine for years, believed that Bodine was an introvert, always trying to prove himself. "Mencken was his god," he said, "and he tried to imitate him in many ways, especially by shocking people." He summed him up as "a combination of Mencken and W. C. Fields." In Bodine's biography I disagreed, saying that such a characterization was oversimplified and did not do him justice. With his ego he did not need a role model, even a Mencken. He was a distinctive personality, truly one of a kind. He said what he honestly believed and he expected people to appreciate his opinions and his honesty. Despite an often gruff manner and enough quirks for seven eccentrics, he was an essentially good-hearted man whose benignity was not always detected. As a small boy Reppert's son Peter made a perceptive observation: "To like Mr. Bodine," he said, "you have to love him."

For friends he would do anything. When *Holiday* was one of the top magazines he was asked to make all the pictures—in color—for a special issue on Maryland. The fee was about $6,000, and this was in 1947. It was an assignment a photographer would dream about. Bodine did not see it that way. He said he would take it on one condition. While editors raised eyebrows in disbelief, he said he would do it if a friend, a young reporter, could write the story on Baltimore which was to be the lead piece. The editors replied that they had a New York writer in mind. Bodine was adamant. They wanted him badly enough to agree to his terms—which is how I came to write the Baltimore profile for *Holiday.*

After his death in October 1970, the Bodine legend continued to flourish. A family that had saved his pictures from the *Sun Magazine* preserved them by decorating the walls of their house. His picture of a mass of docked oyster boats inspired a poem by David Smith which appeared in the *New Yorker* in 1975. It began:

> Aubrey Bodine's crosswater shot of Menchville,
> Virginia; a little dream composing a little water—

An old photograph of his, "The Original Floating Opera," gave John Barth, the noted novelist, the idea for his first book, *The Floating Opera,* already a collector's item. When the *Baltimore News American* asked readers during the bicentennial to select the state's most distinguished citizens, along with the Calverts, Charles Carroll of Carrollton, Francis Scott Key, Edgar Allan Poe, and Johns Hopkins, they named A. Aubrey Bodine. Perhaps the most unusual evocation of his name was in a 1983 obituary. It began, "Memorial services for Miriam Kvarnes, a former swimming instructor who posed for the late A. Aubrey Bodine, will be held . . ." Later it added, "In 1947, Mrs. Kvarnes appeared in *Camera Magazine* in a display of Mr.

Bodine's photographs. She met Mr. Bodine on the beach at Ocean City and posed for him several times. She was also featured in an exhibit of his work at the Smithsonian Institution."

James Thurber began his biography of Harold Ross, founder and editor of the *New Yorker,* with an anecdote illustrating the impact of Ross's restless force and prickly personality. Ross died in December 1951, and the following November the *New Yorker* entertained the editors of *Punch* and some of its writers and artists. Later Thurber told Rowland Emett, the editor of *Punch,* "I'm sorry you didn't get to meet Ross." "Oh, but I did!" Emett replied. "He was all over the place. Nobody talked about anybody else."

Much the same happened after Bodine died. His name, recollections of his work or his piquancies, would pop up in the most unexpected ways. Friends and colleagues, responding to new stimuli, would rue that he wasn't there to explode an opinion they could savor. His thrusting spirit and afterglow were anywhere and everywhere. New members of the staff sometimes thought he must still be around.

Thurber's concluding words of his Ross story are as apt for A. Aubrey Bodine. He "is still all over the place for many of us, vitally stalking the corridors of our lives . . . more evident in death than the living presence of ordinary men."

TWO NUNS, 1935

A. AUBREY BODINE   *The Pictorialist*

In 1920, at the age of fourteen, A. Aubrey Bodine left school and took a job as an errand boy in the Circulation Department of the *Baltimore Sun.* His photographic experience at the time was similar to that of any other teen-ager in the early 1920s—a Kodak box camera and the making of family snapshots. Within four years, he was able to take over the position of commercial photographer in the advertising department. Through ambition and innate talent, he went on to develop a photographic portfolio that enabled him to become *Sunday Sun* photographer in 1927, at the early age of twenty-one. From this position, Bodine attained a national and international reputation as a salon exhibitor and an award-winning newspaper photographer. For almost fifty years, he relentlessly pursued a career as a pictorial photojournalist. It is the interwoven influences of the painterly pictorialist aesthetic and the subject-oriented newspaper profession which form the basis of Bodine's prolific life and his extraordinary photographic legacy.

To fully appreciate Aubrey Bodine's stylistic growth, it is necessary to consider the photographic tradition he entered into in the mid-1920s. With the exception of major cultural centers like New York City, the primary photographic outlet for artistic expression was an informal national network of camera clubs. These clubs were composed of amateur photographers seeking to share ideas and information. The predominant style of the camera clubs was pictorialism.

Pictorialism in photography traces its roots to England and Europe in the 1880s, when "art photographers" sought to separate themselves from the documentary and commercial applications of the medium. The emphasis was on the photographer/artist as a creative individual and on producing a work of art, not a photographic record. The early pictorialists believed that the photographic image should reflect nature as faithfully as possible. Peter Henry Emerson's 1889 manifesto, *Naturalistic Photography,* set forth a doctrine for art photography adopted by the pictorialists. Essential to Emerson's theories was the belief that the straight silver print was too sharp to be naturalistic. Emerson contended that the human eye was incapable of perceiving nature as clearly as the negative could record it; therefore, he advocated soft focus and platinum printing to re-create natural perceptions. In addition to platinum, the pictorialists utilized other nonsilver processes, such as carbro, carbon, bromoil, and gum-bichromate, as well as extensive hand-manipulation of the negative or final print surface—all means intended to heighten the painterly aspects of the photograph.

The overriding ambition of the pictorialist movement was to move photography from the scientific world into the art world. To accomplish this goal, the nineteenth-century pictorialists often looked to painters for inspiration. For increased public awareness of the medium, pictorial photographic exhibitions, or salons, were patterned after the popular painting exhibits. Pictorialists also preferred to receive comments or criticism from contemporary painters and art critics rather than from scientists. Those who championed the artistic theories became the modernists of nineteenth-century photography. In 1892, an ardent group of London pictorialists formed the Linked Ring Brotherhood as a reaction against the academic tenets of the Royal Photographic Society. That same year, Alfred Stieglitz returned to the United States as a leading advocate of pictorialism, stressing its merits for artistic creativity.

Stieglitz's ultimate influence on the direction of twentieth-century painting and photography is well documented. What is pertinent to this essay is his arrival in the United States as a staunch pictorialist photographer with established allegiance to P. H. Emerson and the Linked Ring group. Stieglitz became associated with the Society of Amateur Photographers and, in 1897, a member of the reorganized Camera Club of New York. He edited the club's publication, *Camera Notes,* and organized salon exhibitions he intended to be showcases for pictorialism. By 1902, however, Stieglitz became disillusioned with the conservative attitude and social dogma of the Camera Club. He formed his own small, but now famous, group, the Photo-Session. The original members of Stieglitz's new group were the leading American pictorialists: Edward Steichen, Clarence White, John Bullock, Gertrude Kasebier, Alvin Langdon Coburn (also a member of the Linked Ring), among others. In 1905, with Stieglitz as director, the Photo-Session opened an art gallery at 291 Fifth Avenue and began publication of *Camera Work* to disseminate their pictorialist ideals.

In a little more than ten years, Stieglitz altered his attitude and became a supporter of straight photography, leaving behind the manipulative effects of pictorialism. In his last two issues of *Camera Work,* 1916 and 1917, Stieglitz introduced the photographs of Paul Strand. Strand's theories of straight photography, which emphasized the inherent qualities of the medium,

were diametrically opposed to those of the pictorialists, who continued to look to painters for inspiration. Stieglitz, Strand, and other more formalistic photographers exerted their influence to develop a photographic vocabulary distinct from that of other artistic media. Nevertheless, outside this group of avant-garde thinkers, the pictorialist tradition, and its struggle for acceptance, was perpetuated in the regional camera clubs or within the national Pictorialist Photographers of America.

When A. Aubrey Bodine joined the Photographic Club of Baltimore in 1924, he found a group that was sympathetic to his own artistic intuitions. Established in 1885 and incorporated in 1890, the Baltimore club was one of the early American organizations modeled after European photographic societies. The members met weekly to review each other's photographs and to share information on techniques of developing and printing. The club sponsored its own local salon exhibitions and participated in national and international photographic competitions organized by the Photographic Pictorialists of America, headquartered in New York but not affiliated with the Camera Club of New York or the Stieglitz group. Articles about and theories of pictorialism were published regularly and distributed through the camera clubs. At a time when few schools and universities offered instruction in photography, the camera clubs provided a learning opportunity and a forum for theoretical discussion. Camera club members in Baltimore, as well as other cities, advocated photography as an artistic means of expression. To that end, the amateur photographers continued an admiration for classical painting styles and adhered to the nineteenth-century practices of pictorialism.

Bodine entered his first competition in 1925, with the Photographic Pictorialists of America's New York salon. Two photographs, including "Symphony in Reflections" (p. 2), were accepted for the exhibit. That same year, he won first prize in a Maryland statewide contest for the best set of five prints. Considering his limited educational background and his lack of formal photographic training, the immediate success of his submissions must have been exciting and encouraging to the young man, just nineteen years old. In later years, Bodine expressed a sentimental attachment for "Symphony in Reflections," saying on more than one occasion, "I don't think I've ever done better." Thirty years later, Bodine's photographic archive illustrates that he did do "better," but in no way does that diminish his 1925 achievements.

Bodine's images from the late 1920s and the 1930s are clearly those of a romantic pictorialist. He immediately began experimenting with a variety of approaches, both technical and theoretical, which are associated with the classic style. Finished exhibition prints from this period are predominantly in nonsilver processes, particularly carbro, bromoil, and gum-bichromate, and on a variety of paper surfaces. Heavy manipulation of the negative and final print is evident. Painterly concepts of design and composition are apparent in his work. His images also reflect an effort to emulate the visual results of other artistic mediums, such as drawing and painting. All the basic pictorialist principles are found in Bodine's earliest photographs.

Two rarely published photographs, "Landos vs. Rampher," 1934 (p. 17), and "Boys Swimming in the Patapsco River," 1933 (p. 23), are evidence of Bodine's awareness of painting styles and his photographic antecedents. "Landos vs. Rampher" is a dramatic image of two wrestlers, recalling the popular paintings and drawings of the artist George Bellows (1882–1925). In addition, this particular image was printed in the bromoil process, which required extensive brushwork on the photographic surface and resulted in a final print with the qualities of a lithograph. "Boys Swimming in the Patapsco River" echoes the famous paintings of the Philadelphia artist Thomas Eakins (1844–1916), himself a photographer who frequently used photographs as studies for his paintings. "Boys Swimming" is also reminiscent of the English pictorialist photog-

rapher and member of the Linked Ring, Frank M. Sutcliffe (1859–1940). Sutcliffe produced many photographs of nude young boys swimming or wading among ships in the English harbors. Bodine remarked that he liked this image because he had been able to catch all the boys so they were "decent." Considering the moral climate of Baltimore in the thirties, this is an understandable concern, but certainly not the photograph's primary strength as a work of art. Apparently, Bodine did not consider this image suitable for the rigid criteria of salon judging in the camera clubs. His carefully compiled exhibition record from 1925 through the early 1960s does not list a submission of the photograph. From a 1980s perspective, this is unfortunate. "Boys Swimming in the Patapsco River" is a strong composition capturing many of the inherent properties of an interesting photograph.

The pictorialist doctrine stressed an alliance between art and nature, and often the depiction of man within nature. In his early years, Bodine combined this naturalistic attitude with his affection for and the proximity of the Baltimore Harbor, the Chesapeake Bay, and Maryland's Eastern Shore. "Gloucester Harbor," 1929 (p. 26), and "Chesapeake Bay Skipjack," 1933 (p. 29), vividly illustrate the beginnings of Bodine's visual exploration of his nautical region. Other images at this time are more specifically rooted in pictorialism. "Fort Macon Beach," 1929 (p. 21), contains many of the photographic devices at the heart of traditional pictorialism. A cluster of hooded men lean into the wind, pulling an unseen object from the surf—a symbolic contest with nature. The composition, particularly the figures, is reminiscent of Winslow Homer's (1836–1910) nautical paintings. Areas of the negative have been retouched to deepen the shadows and redefine the outline of the men silhouetted against the clearing sky.

Another characteristic of pictorialism was the ardent desire of amateur photographers to be acknowledged as artists, rather than craftsmen, both publicly through exhibitions and critically in scholarly writing. From his earliest years, Aubrey Bodine was motivated to seek artistic outlets for his work. He was given his first one-man show at the Washington County Museum of Fine Arts in Hagerstown, Maryland, in January of 1933. Elsewhere, with few museums or commercial art galleries expressing curatorial support for photography, the potential for recognition on this level was minimal at best. Various regional photographic organizations made significant efforts in the direction of this goal. Among others, the Buffalo and Pittsburgh camera clubs were respected for the high standards of their salons and publications. In California, the Camera Pictorialists of Los Angeles began working together in 1916, and their 1931 catalogue defined them as "a group of workers who considered that there was more in photography than the production of a negative too perfect, too flawless to ever print." With a highly respected membership including, among others, Will Connell, Imogen Cunningham, Laura Gilpin, Karl Struss, Willard Van Dyke, Brett Weston, and Edward Weston, the California Pictorialists gained recognition through their annual salon exhibitions. Despite such accomplishments on the part of the pictorialists, these events and publications were regional and lacked a centralizing force.

The formation of the national Photographic Society of America (PSA) in 1934 offered the hope of expanded horizons for Aubrey Bodine and thousands of other regional photographers working in relative isolation. Earlier unifying attempts had brought together twenty-two clubs, including the one in Baltimore, under the umbrella of the Associated Camera Clubs of America (ACCA), but had produced no significant results. With the involvement of Dr. Max Thorek from Chicago, the diverse regional interests were combined and the twenty-two members of the ACCA were absorbed into the PSA. The initial functions of the PSA centered on producing a journal to circulate information and pictorialist theories, publicizing nationally the art of photography and standardizing the competitions and

salon exhibitions. The PSA contribution in attempting to elevate the status of amateur photography in America was significant, and it continues today with a worldwide membership of almost fourteen thousand. A. Aubrey Bodine was on the original Board of Governors helping to establish the initial principles of the PSA. He was a consistent participant in the salon competitions and often spoke of the benefits he had reaped from his association with other PSA members.

While the nineteenth-century pictorialists had been considered radicals, those who founded the PSA a half-century later were predominantly conservative, holding fast to the traditional concepts of beauty and romanticism in photography. They saw Beauty and Truth in Nature as the ultimate Good, and the path to Beauty and Truth was a romanticized interpretation of the natural scene recorded on the photographic negative. Frank R. Fraprie, one of the first PSA officers and the editor of the *American Annual of Photography,* wrote in 1935 that "the art of photography is in putting into a photograph more than nature ordinarily offers and giving the beholder food for imagination and thought, as well as the mere mechanical charm of the eye." Romanticized embellishment was at the core of their endeavors.

Other PSA pictorialists adopted a protective attitude toward creating Beauty and reacted against developments in twentieth-century modern art. The organizer and first PSA president, Max Thorek, articulated the orthodox position in his 1939 essay "Sanity in Art." "Since art produced by the camera, which may be called humanity's mechanical eye, is more akin to Nature than is any other human medium of art, every camera artist should strive to the utmost to keep camera art free from profanation." Profanation for Thorek was any form of modernism or experimentation. His views may be regarded as extreme. He was, however, a dominant force in the PSA, and his ideas are a strong indication of the traditional philosophies that dominated the organization in the 1930s.

The concept of unifying a nation of photographers into one cohesive organization proved unworkable. Those photographers who desired Truth or Beauty as the negative presented it to them began to move away from pictorialism. Earlier, in 1932, Willard Van Dyke and Ansel Adams, joined by Edward Weston and others, had founded Group f/64 to take a formalistic stand and to explore the inherent potential of the photographic negative. Even within the original membership of the PSA, alternative voices were being raised. The first issue of the *Journal of the Photographic Society of America,* in January 1935, carried a prophetic message from Nicholas Haz. In a few short paragraphs, Haz succinctly characterized the pictorialists and pleaded for an alternative approach:

To be a pictorialist is still a distinction among photographers in general. A pictorialist has so much respect for painting that he has adopted the painters' code of composition, and is perfectly willing to abandon the peculiar advantages of photography over painting, in order to match or at least to simulate painting-like results. At heart he is a painter who uses the camera instead of the brush, because he had not enough time and perhaps not enough talent to master the brush. But not all photographers are pictorialists. A large number of them could not be, because since they don't know anything about painters' rules they cannot follow them. These are purists because they cannot be anything else. Then there are a few who have been first-rate pictorialists, pathfinders, leaders, makers of history in photography; to mention three: Alfred Stieglitz, Edward J. Steichen, and Edward Weston. Men like these have abandoned their leadership in pictorialism to become mere photographers. These and a few more are determined that now and in the future their pictures will be photographs only; without any admixture of painters' work. . . . Purists are characterized by doing all their thinking about the picture *before* the exposure, since they voluntarily have discarded their freedom to change the picture after it is exposed.

Nicholas Haz called for the formation of a purist group within the Photographic Society of America which would "demonstrate to the world at large that photography is more of an art without than with the painter's help." Apparently, Haz was not able to convert a substantial number of PSA pictorialists to his cause. He may, however, have stimulated some diverse thinking. While Aubrey Bodine never abandoned pictorialism, he did assimilate some purist approaches into his work, particularly in the area of preconceptualizing the photograph he was making. Bodine's affiliation with photojournalism was the contributing influence in any deviations he made from the absolute doctrine of pictorialism.

In 1927, Aubrey Bodine's new position on the staff of the *Sunday Sun* thrust him into the photojournalistic milieu, a profession and style with its roots in straight, or pure, photography. The basic principles of photojournalism, that is, visual reporting, are in conflict with the practices of a romantic pictorialist. As the Sunday feature photographer, Bodine faced no necessity to adhere to the strict concepts of photojournalism. His early images found an audience in the *Sun*'s readership which responded enthusiastically to his personal brand of romanticized reportage. Combining idealized interpretation with journalistic reporting, Bodine established a mode of artistic expression which he was to develop and refine throughout the balance of his career. It was this personal vision that set him apart from both his fellow PSA members and his colleagues in photojournalism. With the nation suffering an economic depression and heading toward a world war, Bodine's photographic view of the world around him offered a respite from harsh reality. At the same time, he believed his challenge was to elevate photography in the art world. The *Baltimore Sun* was his vehicle, the photographic salons his arena.

By the end of his first decade at the *Sun,* Bodine was firmly established with the Photographic Society of America as an award-winning pictorialist exhibitor. He took pride in his 1936 election as associate member of the Pittsburgh Camera Club, and he served as a judge for salon competitions in other East Coast cities. His work also gained visibility outside the confines of Baltimore and the PSA. Bodine images appeared in the first three issues of *U.S. Camera:* "Two Nuns" (p. 10) in the 1935 premiere publication, an untitled industrial image in 1936, and "Contour Plowing" (p. 31) in 1937. Organized in New York, with T. J. Maloney as editor and the eminent Edward Steichen guiding the selection of images, *U.S. Camera* contained full-page illustrations by little-known amateurs as well as highly respected professional photographers. Bodine was represented among an impressive cross section of the photographic elite, notably, Cecil Beaton, Dorothea Lange, Berenice Abbott, Imogen Cunningham, George Hurrell, Margaret Bourke-White, Henri Cartier-Bresson, Edward Weston, and Brett Weston. This exposure attracted the attention of editors at *Harper's* and *Look* and potentially could have led to wider recognition for his work.

Regrettably, Bodine had neither the temperament nor the inclination to take advantage of this opportunity. His employment at the *Baltimore Sun* and his private commercial accounts required his full attention. In addition, he was suffering from the effects of professional and personal pressure, combined with the debilitating consequences of alcoholism. To his credit, Bodine conquered his depression (totally abstaining from alcohol for the rest of his life), and in early 1942, after a short period of hospitalization, he regained his former level of productivity. By that time, however, World War II had become the dominant subject of photographic publications in New York, and Bodine was preoccupied with the responsibilities of his promotion to head of the photographic department of the *Sunday Sun.* He spent the balance of his professional career documenting the mid-Atlantic states for the pleasure of his Baltimore followers and his salon companions.

LANDOS VS. RAMPHER, 1934

DOCK WORKERS, 1925

18

STUDY IN ANGLES, 1924

OVERHAULING THE MARINER'S FRIEND, 1931

FORT MACON BEACH, 1929

WIND SWEPT CORN STALKS, 1934

BOYS SWIMMING IN THE PATAPSCO RIVER, 1933

ROOF TOPS, NUREMBERG, 1930

CAMBRIDGE, 1929

GLOUCESTER HARBOR, 1929

PILING COPPER CAKES, 1934

GLOUCESTER DOCK, 1929

CHESAPEAKE BAY SKIPJACK, 1933

CONOWINGO DAM, 1936

30

CONTOUR PLOWING, 1937

MAIN SAIL, DORIS HAMLIN, 1939

A. AUBREY BODINE *The Continuing Career*

With the end of World War II, A. Aubrey Bodine had settled into the professional routine he was to pursue relentlessly until the complications of diabetes slowed his pace in the mid-1960s. On the personal side, he had overcome his earlier illness and depression, married Nancy Tait (an earlier marriage had ended in divorce), and established a secure family life with his stepdaughter, Stuart, and his daughter, Jennifer, born in 1948.

Bodine's photographic activities were concentrated on three distinct, but inseparable, affiliations: the *Baltimore Sunday Sun*, the Photographic Society of America (PSA), and the National Press Photographers Association (NPPA). As feature photographer for the *Sunday Sun*, Bodine became, by definition, a photojournalist, but one with an audience to be entertained as well as informed. Conversely, he established a loyalty to the pictorialist philosophies of the PSA, submitting for salon scrutiny images that had been produced while on assignment for the *Sun*. In the NPPA, he perpetuated the enigma by presenting salon photographs for review among hard-core journalists. Each endeavor was approached with enthusiasm and almost manic energy. As he had begun in the early years, Bodine continued to merge the influences of romantic pictorialism and photojournalism with his own idiosyncrasies. The final product of his curious mixture was an extraordinary photographic heritage.

A. AUBREY BODINE
and the *Baltimore Sun*

Bodine described the manner in which he combined photojournalism for the *Baltimore Sun* with his desire to participate in the pictorialist salons: "I try to cover assignments in such a way as to have something available for exhibition. Competition with other amateurs keeps me on my toes and helps me keep my newspaper work up to snuff. If it were not for my salon work, I would not put half as much effort into each newspaper assignment. Salons are a goal I enjoy shooting at." He also proclaimed, "There is no difference between my salon prints and news pictures."

When the Sunday newspaper format changed and the first issue of the *Sun Magazine* appeared in January 1946, Bodine's photographs were featured in an article applauding the International Salon of Photography on view at the Baltimore Museum. The new magazine made extensive use of photography in the layout. Although there were other photographers on the staff, Bodine was given preferential treatment, and his work appeared with the greatest regularity. The magazine editors realized the appeal of his pictorial style and allowed him great latitude in his activities. While he often accompanied reporters to cover stories and did fulfill specific editorial assignments, his personal input on the final picture selection and design was often apparent.

A poignant portrait of a Yugoslav woman ("Emigrant Woman," p. 44) appeared as the cover of a 1948 issue to introduce a story on increased immigration to Baltimore. In fact, the portrait had been taken as early as 1939. Whether or not the editors were aware of the time frame is irrelevant. For Bodine, the image worked in the context of the story and he used it.

Sun Magazine editor Neil Swanson conceived of the Maryland Gallery, "a series of full-page photographs of Maryland scenes that will appear as a weekly feature for an indefinite period." The first Maryland Gallery appeared on December 5, 1948, and was, as the premiere article explains, Bodine's gallery: "These pictures are more than photographs. They are Bodines—genuine works of art produced over a period of twenty years by A. Aubrey Bodine, photographic director of the Magazine. Many of them have repeatedly taken honors in international salon exhibitions. Because of their beauty and distinction, these pictures will undoubtedly appeal to many persons as subjects for framing and permanent preservation."

The *Sun* was obviously proud of Aubrey Bodine and his prize-winning photographs. What is more, the public loved it. Six months later, a follow-up story appeared detailing the popularity of the Maryland Gallery and its value as a "pictorial record" of the Maryland countryside and as an education to amateur photographers. One reader wrote the *Sun* saying, "The pictures have the same effect on me as musical masterpieces. On rainy days I look at them for hours and they cheer me up wonderfully."

In 1984, I received a phone call at my Washington, D.C., art gallery from a gentleman who had just bought a house in the Baltimore suburbs. He was asking for professional advice because one room of his new home had been wallpapered with Bodine photographs. He wanted to know their value before he painted or ripped them off the walls. Mystified and intrigued by the possibility of a small fortune in Bodine photographs landing in my lap, I pressed the caller for more information. "Listen lady," he said, "I tell you I'm sitting in a room that is fifteen feet long and twelve feet wide and it's wallpapered from floor to ceiling with Bodine photographs. There must be over two hundred of them and they're all signed. What should I do with this room?" As it turned out, the wallpaper was made up of pages from the Maryland Gallery. The previous owner had created his own shrine to A. Aubrey Bodine.

The Maryland Gallery continued monthly for many years, utilizing Bodine images that were originally intended for salon exhibitions. Even in the late sixties, when Bodine was not physically able to complete regular assignments, full-page Bodine images still appeared for purely decorative purposes in the *Magazine*. Few, if any, photojournalists have been honored with such extensive exposure on the pages of a weekly publication.

In addition to contributing to the Maryland Gallery, Bodine, as head of the photographic department, worked directly with the editors and writers and completed weekly assignments for the *Magazine*. His life was spent traveling the states of Maryland, Pennsylvania, and Virginia gathering photographs for story illustrations. The editors were aware of his impatient temperament and his professed dislike of making portraits. Although the majority of his projects were scenes of the rural landscapes or the harbor and bay areas, Bodine did produce many remarkable portraits. As he traveled the region for the *Sun*, he developed a rapport with traditionally unapproachable social groups, such as the rugged watermen of the Chesapeake Bay or the reclusive Amish colonies. "The Gentle People" (p. 70) is an endearing study of young Amish girls. Bodine's portraits of Eastern Shore watermen and tradesmen are evidence of a similar affinity. Perhaps he sympathized with their endurance and ability to perpetuate a romantic lifestyle of sailmaking, blacksmithing, or harvesting oysters under sail in all types of weather. Whatever his reasons, some of his most dramatic photographs and portraits are of the Chesapeake Bay and the people for whom the region provided a way of life.

A. AUBREY BODINE
and the Photographic Society of America

Throughout his photojournalistic career, Aubrey Bodine believed pictorial effects enhanced news photography. In 1946, he was quoted as saying that "it is easy to spot a newspaper photographer who has had some art training or is interested in pictorial photography. It quickly reflects in his work and editors are eager to use pictures which have excellent print quality and dramatic impact." The *Sunday Sun* editors reinforced Bodine's theory with their encouragement and frequent publication of his salon-style images. Bodine's mastery of pictorialist techniques was accomplished by means of his lifelong involvement in salon competitions and the activities of the Photographic Society of America.

In Bodine's time, the PSA salon exhibitions were a means of overcoming regional isolation within a diverse geographic membership. In addition to satisfying the natural instinct of sharing one's photographic accomplishments, the experience provided a vehicle for the exchange of ideas and for self-improvement. By the 1940s, in an effort toward universal fairness, the PSA had devised a system of standardization for salon competitions and exhibitions. Contestants were to enter no more than four prints into officially recognized salons. Entries were restricted on the theory that photographers would produce better pictures by concentrating on a relatively small number of finished prints. Prints submitted were separated during the review, guaranteeing that each would be considered on its individual merits rather than as part of a portfolio. The judges were selected from within the PSA membership and were previous salon winners. As many as twelve judges reviewed each photograph as it was placed under controlled lighting in a black viewing stand of a PSA-recommended size and light intensity. Sitting at a distance of ten feet and without comment, the judges raised a paddle, voting the print in or out of the salon exhibit.

Initially the salon system was perceived as one that would encourage quality, not quantity, submissions. Ultimately, the rules became so rigid that Bodine and others like him protested loudly. Bodine published an essay entitled "Evils of Present Day Judging" in the June 1943 issue of the monthly PSA *Journal.* Bodine, himself a judge and regular winner under the existing system, counseled for three specific changes: revising the viewing stand, eliminating silent voting, and reducing the size of juries. He recommended a three-man jury with an open discussion of the photographs reviewed and a viewing stand of a neutral color. He believed that photographers would benefit from a debate on the photograph's merits or deficiencies, therefore aiding self-improvement. Bodine pointed out that art galleries and studios did not have black walls. He felt "the result of using a dark background is that delicate and lovely tones are destroyed, for they were never made to be seen under such conditions." Eventually two of his recommendations were accepted for the salons, but the black viewing stand is still used in many current camera club competitions.

Other voices against the system were heard. To its credit, the PSA was at least willing to consider the objections. The November 1948 PSA *Journal* featured Ansel Adams' warnings against the salon process. Adams, a PSA member, said that "prints are made for what the photographers think may be the composite taste of the salon judges, not for the satisfaction of the inner being of the photographer." Aubrey Bodine was never an admirer of Ansel Adams; their theories and practices—one a romantic pictorialist, the other a purist—were incompatible. Nevertheless, they were in complete agreement in their attitude toward PSA salons. Bodine echoed Adams' sentiment by saying, "One merely has to watch the shows to find out what clicks and then duplicate the subject matter and technique."

Although he was a member of the PSA, there is no evidence that Adams ever competed in the salons. Bodine competed consistently and his feelings were based on firsthand experience. His famous image "Choptank Oyster Dredgers" (p. 53) had won first prize in the 1948 Popular Photography national competition, selected from over fifty-one thousand entries. Yet when this stunning image was submitted to a camera club salon in Boston, Bodine received the following written comment from a respected judge. "While the figures in the boat are rather static and their arrangement is not the happiest, especially the two dominant figures which overlap each other, the mood of the squally, rainy day is well rendered." The judge was Frank R. Fraprie, one of the highest rated salon competitors as well as an author and editor of many pictorial publications. The salon system necessitated criticism, no matter how gratuitous it might be. Situations similar to this may have inspired Bodine to make his most emotional plea for salon reform, in a 1949 letter to a PSA colleague. "The calibre of judges is so low it is a national disgrace." In words characteristic of Bodine's opinionated manner, he continued: "It is time to stop incompetent people from judging who in most cases are businessmen successfully earning their living in law, medicine, salesmanship, etc. Even though I know enough to take care of my belly aches (except this one) I am thankful that there are laws prohibiting me from practicing medicine." Bodine complained further, "During my quarter century of exhibiting, I have struggled along with others to have major art museums accept photography. In the last decade I have seen them one by one pushing out Salons, whose fault is this??—those who are assuming an active part in Salon photography. . . . In order to raise the standard we should absolutely insist on at least one artist on the jury."

A. Aubrey Bodine's sentiments were heard and his influence was felt. In 1951, the Baltimore Museum of Art discontinued its sponsorship of the annual Baltimore Camera Club salon, complaining that the exhibit was monotonous, repetitious, and imitative of past salons. The following year, however, the museum renewed its participation when the club agreed to a jury of three

prominent artists, not photographers. In his article "Is Pictorial Photography Dying?" Bodine applauded what he called the "Baltimore Experiment," labeling the show a success because of the jury of artists and the elimination of the rule requiring acceptance of no fewer than 125 prints. Two of his photographs had been rejected and he agreed with the decision of the judges. Bodine saw the Baltimore show as an opportunity for fresh ideas. "As perhaps the old guard fails to realize, surely the new generation will discover it takes more than perfect technique to make a picture." He concluded his essay by saying, "What we need most is freedom of expression and not the suppression of new ideas and concepts."

Competition was, and in many areas still is, one of the most important activities in the PSA camera clubs. The *American Annual of Photography* published a yearly *Who's Who in Pictorial Photography,* an international listing of the members enumerating the number of salons to which they had submitted and the number of prints accepted. Some photographers submitted prints to as many as eighty-five individual salons in one year. The task of preparing, packaging, and shipping their prints around the world could easily turn a hobby into a time-consuming occupation. Bodine generally sent photographs to between twenty and thirty salons, and then only the major ones. As much as he enjoyed the participation and the competition, he hated being bothered with preparing the forms and making the shipments. His wife, Nancy, was in charge of the salon submissions. Their combined efforts were rewarded, as Bodine's percentage of acceptances was always very high and the camera clubs welcomed his cooperation.

The *American Annual of Photography* also calculated the numerical standing of the most prolific exhibitors as well as a rating, similar to a batting average, determined by the average number of prints in each salon. To reach this level of accomplishment, rivalry within the local clubs was inevitable. Aubrey Bodine once admired a

Reverse of "Overhauling the Mariner's Friend" (p. 20). Once a photograph was accepted for a PSA salon, a decorative exhibition stamp or label was placed on the back of the photographic mount. Particularly successful photographs, like this one, often ended up with layers of labels providing a travelogue of the photograph's exhibition history. The shows that resulted from the salon judgings were often displayed in a local art museum or library for public viewing. In such exhibits, Bodine's photographs were acquired for the permanent collections of the Seattle Art Museum, the Detroit Institute of Arts, and the Toronto Museum of Art. The earliest show date on this photograph is 1931, in Pittsburgh, and the latest is 1945, in Omaha.

photograph by fellow club member Edward Bafford and asked for the location of the tree-lined lane in the image. At first Bafford was reluctant to disclose the site. Bodine persisted and Bafford finally gave him directions. Once on the scene, Bodine placed his camera in every possible position, trying to reconstruct Bafford's point of view. Unsuccessful and frustrated, Bodine confronted Bafford again, demanding an explanation. Finally, Bafford was forced to admit that after he had exposed the negative, he cut down the tree limb framing the image so that no one, especially Bodine, could attempt to duplicate his success.

For A. Aubrey Bodine, photography was not a hobby; it was a profession to which he was devoted. Despite all his complaints, justified as they might have been, he continued to submit photographs to the PSA salons, concentrating on international exhibits after 1955. Bodine's PSA associate Frank Christopher arranged for his work to be included in the first exhibit of United States photographers sent to Moscow in 1961. "Longshoremen" (p. 87) was well received and won a silver medal in the Soviet capital. A one-man show of Bodine photographs was also circulated throughout Eastern and Western Europe. Bodine repeatedly expressed his belief that he had received more benefits from the PSA salons and the people he met through them than from any other single area of his photographic involvements. "I cannot emphasize too strongly how much I have derived from pictorial exhibition work. The many fine people whom I have met over a period of years are a never-ending source of pleasure. I have reaped many benefits, too numerable to mention. In return I have attempted to show my appreciation by lecturing and giving continual support to salons, whether they be big or small." In 1965, the PSA acknowledged his efforts and elected him an Honorary Fellow of the Society in recognition of "his talent, accomplishments and encouraging influence in photography as an art and his devoted service to the PSA over a long period." Bodine was understandably proud of his achievements in the Photographic Society of America.

A. AUBREY BODINE
and the National Press Photographers Association

The National Press Photographers Association began with a 1945 conference of eighteen respected photographers from the leading newspapers in the country. A. Aubrey Bodine represented the *Baltimore Sun* and worked closely with the first NPPA president, Joseph Costa, a *New York Daily News* photographer, in the formation of a national organization to promote respect and recognition for the profession of photojournalism. Joseph Costa is still active in the field at eighty-one years of age (retiring in 1985 from teaching photojournalism at Ball State University in Muncie, Indiana). He remembers that Bodine "was a fine pictorialist and very influential in the early days of the NPPA." "Bodine," Costa says, "was always positive in his opinions and did not hesitate to express them." The concept of a

national umbrella for press photographers took hold, and within the first year participation in the NPPA grew from the original eighteen charter members to 667 photographers, reaching twelve hundred by 1947. The National Press Photographers Association currently boasts eight thousand members, a record enrollment for NPPA, and operates with an annual budget of over half a million dollars.

In the April 1946 first edition of the NPPA newsletter, an editorial called for "equal rights for photographers," specifically in relationship to their colleagues in the writing press. In the mid-forties, press photographers were essentially self-trained, intuitive "shooters," working without the benefit, or refinements, of formal education. The advent of a national organization provided a lobbying potential for their branch of journalism which had not been attainable by the fragmented regional press photographers groups. The two other dominating concerns of the early NPPA were access to courtroom proceedings for photographers and protection for their members from physical attacks and abuse on the part of the public, who perceived press photographers as aggressive intruders.

Aubrey Bodine's position with the *Baltimore Sun* set him apart from the majority of NPPA members. Bodine was a feature photographer working with the respect of the *Sun* reporters and with the advantage of an adoring public that was thrilled when Bodine arrived to take a picture. He had none of the daily pressures to produce timely "spot" news photos. The *Sunday Sun* editors were willing to give him enormous flexibility with photo assignments. And yet, Bodine enthusiastically participated in the initial stages of the NPPA, gained the respect of his colleagues, and continued an active involvement for over twenty years.

Bodine admitted his particular place in photojournalism. "Newspaper photography has always been my work, although not in the sense that most people think of newspaper photography, as I do only feature work for the *Baltimore*

Sunday Sun." Later he said, "I do not cover fires or anyone bitten by a dog—I have never worked on the daily end of a paper, only Sunday work." With his popularity well established and his *Sun* job secure, Bodine had channeled his competitive instincts into the salons of the Photographic Society of America. When, in 1948, the NPPA began its annual awards for photographic achievements, Bodine was faced with a new challenge. Stepping out of a romantic pictorialist tradition, he now found his images pitted against documents of hard news issues. Although published in a newspaper, Bodine's photographs were from a different genre. Other feature photographers must have shared his sentiments of frustration. The 1948 "Best Picture of My Life" NPPA contest was won by Associated Press photographer Murray Becker for his dramatic shot of the dirigible *Hindenburg* burning at Lakehurst, New Jersey, on May 5, 1937.

The Press Photographers of Baltimore, Inc., was formed and sponsored its first annual exhibition in 1947 "to give the public an opportunity to see enlarged prints of the pictures which appear in the newspapers, artistically toned and mounted in salon style." Consistent with his salon record, Bodine won two awards in this first show. In the local Baltimore setting Bodine was recognized for his feature accomplishments with a first prize in the pictorial and the personality categories.

In the first three years of NPPA annual awards, there were no category divisions of subject matter. All photos submitted were given equal consideration, subdivided only by the circulation size of the journal in which they had been published. Despite Bodine's success in the PSA and in Baltimore, national recognition from his peers in photojournalism was not immediate.

It was certainly no coincidence that in 1951, when the rules were changed to broaden the categories allowing competitive opportunity to a wider range of photojournalists, Aubrey Bodine was chairman of the NPPA Photo Contest Committee. In addition to the awards based on the circulation of the contestant's newspaper, seven new subdivisions were created to receive awards: Spot News, Feature, Pictorial, Color, Personalities, Sports, and Speedlight (flash). With steadfast persistence, Bodine brought his artistic salon experience into the world of photojournalism. In the 1952 contest, he received second- and third-place awards in the Pictorial Division. With slight variations, the category headings initiated by Bodine are still used by the NPPA in its annual competition.

In 1953, a Portfolio Class was added to judge the photographer on more than a single image, and the venerable title "Newspaper Photographer of the Year" was inaugurated. Ironically, Bodine's rival on the *Sunday Sun,* Hans Marx, won the 1953 award as Newspaper Photographer of the Year. Bodine's talents, however, did not go unrecognized. He won first prize in the Portraits and Personalities category ("The Gentle People," p. 70) as well as first and second in Pictorial. That same year, Bodine was awarded a NPPA Fellowship "in recognition of his outstanding achievement as photographer, pictorialist and exhibitor in photographic salons throughout the world and for the attention and recognition which such success has brought to the profession of photojournalism."

The title "Newspaper Photographer of the Year" remained his goal. Finally, in 1957, Bodine was named "Newspaper-Magazine Photographer of the Year," a distinction created by the judges specifically for A. Aubrey Bodine. The NPPA April 1957 newsletter elaborated on the new award: "Bodine had the highest point score in the whole competition. He was highest both on the straight point basis on which the contest was judged and on the basis of pictures receiving prizes or being accepted for the travelling exhibit in the individual categories. However, the judges felt a distinction had to be made between a photographer covering assignments for Sunday feature use like Bodine, and one covering general assignments—daily spot-news events." Bodine was infuriated and refused to accept the decision.

Joseph Costa confirms Bodine's annoyance. "He was adamant there should not have been a distinction between newspaper magazine and daily newspaper work." Bodine continued to support the NPPA activities, entering and constantly winning awards in the annual contests. Regardless, he never acknowledged that he was anything other than the 1957 "Newspaper Photographer of the Year."

A. AUBREY BODINE
and His Techniques

Aubrey Bodine's entire adult life was devoted to his photography. He worked long days with regularity, preferring to leave home early and spending hours setting up or waiting for the precise moment to expose his negative. Many photographers have followed a similar routine. The ultimate question remains: What did he do to make his photographs stand out among those of the many pictorialists and photojournalists in his field?

With his colleagues, Bodine developed a reputation for being secretive about his techniques, both in taking the picture and in printing it in the darkroom. Competitiveness, particularly within the Baltimore Camera Club, is one explanation for this assessment. Another possibility is that he did a great deal of experimentation and did not want anyone in the darkroom with him hanging over his shoulder. His friend and fellow *Sun* photographer Richard Stacks, now a commercial photographer in San Francisco, confirms Bodine's reticence to openly discuss his darkroom procedures. Although their offices were next door to each other's, Stacks says Bodine never divulged the process he used behind the closed door. Stacks never saw him actually printing a photograph. "When other photographers found out I knew Bodine, they thought I would also know his secrets. He never told me anything." In fact, Bodine did, in personal correspondence and in publications, give a great deal of information about what he was doing in the darkroom.

From his personal papers, interviews, and the articles he published, it is apparent that Bodine was willing to communicate about his methods and formulas. He was particularly fond of the gum-bichromate process, having researched the technique thoroughly, and he spoke of publishing a book on his findings. He used view camera equipment, 4×5 and 5×7 formats, and he regularly gave advice regarding potential films and developers. He also recommended photographing in the early morning or late afternoon when the light is soft.

Bodine once said, "To describe print quality in detail would be like describing a beautiful woman—both should be the zenith of perfection." To achieve his concept of perfection, Bodine insisted on a full tonal range in printing, from "dark shadows through the middle tones up to the highlights which should have detail—in other words, no chalky white areas." In keeping with his pictorialist training, he believed that "the picture is more dramatic and carries more impact if the darkest shadows or areas are completely dark." He liked mixing old developer with fresh developer. "This will produce a print with more pronounced warm tones—almost olive." The final stage of printing, toning the print with selenium, sulphide, or—his favorite—gold toner, was an essential part of Bodine's process. It was also the most intrusive of his photographic habits for his family. He would develop and print the images in his darkroom at the *Baltimore Sun*. Then he would bring all the material home for toning. The bathtub was filled with prints soaking in toner, and the dining room table and floor were his drying racks.

There are many indications of extensive retouching on the photographic print surface. Writing in 1950 Bodine outlined the finishing touches with the following details: "After the print is dry a sharp etching knife should be used to remove pin hole spots, etc. Water color such as Windsor Newton or Webers used to cover up the white spots. Finally, wax, varnish or use print lustre which will not remove the retouching but

"Rowing at Ebb Tide," before extensive brushwork on the negative removed the small rowboat and two pilings on the left.

will hide all indications of spotting. This will bring back the brilliancy that the print had when it was wet. Most of the print lustre solutions are too thick, so use some turpentine as a thinner."

Bodine did tell how he made his exposures and gave advice on chemicals and papers. What he was not able to convey in words was his special talent for altering or manipulating the negative film. With the skill and delicacy of a painter, he used a thin brush and red dye to emphasize highlights and redefine subjects. In "Pennsylvania Train Yard, Baltimore" (p. 73), the smoke billowing in the sky has been accentuated with extensive brush work. "Rowing at Ebb Tide" (p. 63) is one of the most vivid examples of his ability to completely change a negative to achieve pictorialist perfection. The illustration

printed here is from the original negative, before Bodine removed the boat and dark pilings on the left. He also found the composition more satisfactory when he flopped the negative, placing the dominant figure of the man in a rowboat on the left. For several of his favorite prints, Bodine would reverse the negative to improve the composition. To produce the master print, there were no limits to Bodine's imagination and inventiveness.

Bodine was known to keep files of cloud negatives to be added to his exhibition prints of landscapes or water scenes. As an avowed pictorialist, he developed this technique out of a well-established tradition. Nineteenth-century naturalistic photographers were handicapped by negative material that lacked the color sensitivity

"Corn Fields, Frederick County, Maryland."

simultaneously to record the subtle cloud forma-tions and the darker shadow areas of landscape. To compensate for the limitations of the materials, these photographers began exposing negatives that contained only clouds and then double printing the final image, first for the landscape and then for the cloud detail. This practice, initiated out of technical necessity, was quickly adopted by the pictorialists as one of many devices for increased romanticism.

Pictorialist journals regularly featured articles espousing the benefits of adding clouds to pic-tures. Among the books in Bodine's library was the 1935 *American Annual of Photography,* in which H. W. Honess Lee advocated the extensive use of clouds. Lee theorized that "success in picture-making is largely dependent upon knowl-edge and resource in the matter of skies." Further, he reasoned, "the composition of a picture can be

completely changed by the introduction of a well-defined cloud." Bodine made no secret of his use of cloud negatives. "For years," he wrote to an admirer, "I have been successfully printing in clouds and think nothing of printing clouds on regular routine assignments." Even in his role as a photojournalist, Bodine advocated the addition of clouds. With such a technique he could also change the mood or even the time of day in an image. A water scene printed with heavy clouds would appear to be from a negative taken late in the day. The same negative could be printed with lighter clouds and give the appearance of morn-ing or early afternoon. The landscape cited here illustrates Bodine's inclination to experiment with potential compositions. The cloud formations in "Corn Fields, Frederick County, Maryland" are the same ones that appear in several different landscapes: "Springtime, Nova Scotia" (p. 82) and "October Fields, Baltimore County, Maryland" (p. 71) are two examples.

Clouds were not the only elements Bodine added to his photographs. Silhouettes of birds, particularly seagulls, were sometimes added to water scenes as a compositional enhancement. To create a well-defined moon or sun, Bodine may have painted the negative or placed an appropriate size coin on the paper during the darkroom exposure. He liked to add specks of white to simulate snow or rain in his photographs, frequently on the overall image, or, in many instances, simply on certain areas. The snow piled on the ironwork in "Fells Point, Baltimore" (p. 88) was totally added in the darkroom. When he wanted more moonlight reflecting on the water or when he felt additional white highlights would be an improvement, he used his brush and dye to paint the details onto the negative. Often, to create a window or frame, he would add fish nets to the final image. The nets of "Devil's Island" (p. 93) were printed over the original negative of the docked sailboats and are characteristic of his frequent net technique.

In the final analysis, A. Aubrey Bodine did whatever he wanted and took any number of liberties with the photographic negative and print. All his efforts were concentrated on the creation of a beautiful photograph, the pictorialist ideal. During the 1950s and 1960s, at the height of his career, curators and scholars were focusing their attention on exploring the inherent formalistic qualities of photography. Pictorialism was considered derivative and was relegated to the history books. Bodine's eye did mature, and images such as "Beggar at Howard and Lexington Streets, Baltimore" (p. 97) indicate his awareness of modern trends. Still, he was justifiably considered a regional pictorialist.

Over the past decade, contemporary photographers have reappraised the fundamental ingredients of pictorialism. Exhibitions and publications have been devoted to the nonsilver or hand-applied emulsion processes. Multiple printing and manipulation of the negative or print surface is seen with regularity. The division between photography and the other artistic activities of painting and of printmaking is no longer strictly defined. Renowned painters such as David Hockney and Robert Rauschenberg make headlines with their exploration into the photographic medium. Established photographers are working more and more with painterly techniques, demonstrating their freedom and affirming their legitimate claim for artistic recognition.

A. Aubrey Bodine was a photographic enigma. He successfully managed to balance his attachment to a nineteenth-century aesthetic with the daily requirements of a photojournalist. He was an extraordinary photographic technician who continually experimented with his medium to produce better prints and who maintained worldwide visibility through his professional outlets at the *Baltimore Sun* and with the PSA and the NPPA. And yet, he refused to involve himself with any of the trends or explorations that took place in photography during the course of his career. Although he had one foot placed firmly in a pictorialist tradition, his mid-twentieth-century images foretell a return to the basic concepts of romanticism.

After several years of ill health, Bodine suffered a stroke in his darkroom at the *Sun*. He died in 1970 before he had a chance to witness and to share in a revival and reevaluation of the style he had pursued with unfaltering devotion—pictorialism.

EMIGRANT WOMAN, 1939

H. L. MENCKEN, CIRCA 1940

ICED IN, SPA CREEK, ANNAPOLIS, MARYLAND, 1936

CURVING STEPS, 1943

OYSTER TONGER, 1948

BIRCHES, VERMONT, 1946

OCEAN CITY FISH DOCK, CIRCA 1955

CHESAPEAKE BAY SKIPJACKS, CIRCA 1955

CHOPTANK OYSTER DREDGERS, 1948

SKIPJACK MAKING A LICK, CIRCA 1955

SAILMAKER, ALBERT BROWN, 1954

CHESAPEAKE BAY WATERMAN, 1953

MELVIN COLLIER, DEAL ISLAND BLACKSMITH, CIRCA 1950

RAKING CLAMS, 1948

GWYNN'S ISLAND, 1948

SPRING WHEAT FIELD, CHARLES COUNTY, MARYLAND, 1948

OXEN, CALVERT COUNTY, MARYLAND, 1953

ROWING AT EBB TIDE, 1944

AMISH BOYS, 1952

THE WARD BROTHERS, CIRCA 1950

CRAB DREDGING, CIRCA 1955

DEAL ISLAND DEAD-RISE CRAB SKIFF, CIRCA 1955

FISHERMAN, LOCH RAVEN, 1950

POCOMOKE RIVER, WORCESTER COUNTY, MARYLAND, 1950

THE GENTLE PEOPLE, 1952

OCTOBER FIELDS, BALTIMORE COUNTY, MARYLAND, 1949

BESSEMER CONVERTER, BETHLEHEM STEEL, SPARROWS POINT, 1946

PENNSYLVANIA TRAIN YARD, BALTIMORE, CIRCA 1945

INDUSTRIAL POWER, 1950

BLAST FURNACES, SPARROWS POINT, 1946

BARNS, LIBERTY ROAD, 1943

AMISH WOMAN, 1960

H. L. MENCKEN, 1955

GATHERING MAPLE SAP, 1950

MAINE COAST, 1952

SPRINGTIME, NOVA SCOTIA, 1952

NETS, NOVA SCOTIA, 1952

BALTIMORE HARBOR, NIGHT, 1949

SHIP CHANDLER'S WINDOW, CIRCA 1955

BALTIMORE HARBOR, 1955

LONGSHOREMEN, 1955

FELLS POINT, BALTIMORE, 1950

LONG DOCK, BALTIMORE HARBOR, 1947

LONG HAUL, MAINE, 1952

TANGIERS SOUND, CRISFIELD, MARYLAND, 1948

DEVIL'S ISLAND, 1961

TOBACCO FIELD, 1947

CHECKERS GAME, CRISFIELD, MARYLAND, CIRCA 1960

PALMISTRY WINDOW, CIRCA 1960

BEGGAR AT HOWARD AND LEXINGTON STREETS, BALTIMORE, 1968

NOTES ON THE PHOTOGRAPHS

From the time he made his first exhibition print in 1924 until the end of his career in 1970, A. Aubrey Bodine photographed almost daily for his newspaper, the *Baltimore Sun,* and for his own pleasure. The sheer volume of his production is staggering. Approximately six thousand negatives have been donated to the Mariner's Museum in Newport News, Virginia, and over ten thousand are in the collection of the Peale Museum in Baltimore, Maryland. The photographs selected for this publication were chosen to illustrate his best images as well as the vast range of his visual interests. Some photographs are favorite Bodine pictures and were published in his books and other journals; some have not been seen since the 1930s and early 1940s.

Bodine printed and exhibited his photographs extensively over many years, making the task of tracing and accurately dating the images difficult. The earliest known exhibition or publication dates are used in this index. Over the years, pictures appeared with various titles, sometimes the work of an editor's pen, often the result of the photographer's humor and imagination. Whenever possible, Bodine's own titles have been used to describe the images. Most of the photographs were printed on standard silver paper and then toned with a variety of chemical combinations. Examples of unusual printing techniques are cited. Bodine photographs have been acquired for numerous public and private collections across the country. Credit is given to some of the significant museums or collections

that possess unique prints. Not every photograph required elaboration and not all collections are noted. While every attempt has been made at thoroughness and accuracy, the illustrations and this list are not intended to be comprehensive.

Page 2. "Symphony in Reflections," 1925. Although first shown in 1925, this image remained one of Bodine's favorites. Made during his early years, it was exhibited in 1926 at the Paris International Salon, acquired for the permanent collection at Toronto in 1927, and received first place in 1929 at the Chicago Art Institute.

Page 10. "Two Nuns," 1935. The effect of falling snow was achieved by drawing on the negative. In addition to other awards, this photograph won a gold medal at the 1955 Hong Kong salon. "Two Nuns" is in the permanent collection of the Fogg Museum, Harvard University.

Page 17. "Landos vs. Rampher," 1934. Jim Landos was a prize-winning wrestler in the 1930s. The only known example of the image is a bromoil print now in the photographic collection of the J. Paul Getty Museum, Santa Monica, California.

Page 18. "Dock Workers," 1925. The photograph was taken on Pratt Street in the Baltimore Harbor.

Page 19. "Study in Angles," 1924. One of the men in the photograph is Holmes Mettee, a portrait photographer in Baltimore who took the frontispiece photograph of Bodine. The original print of this image is in the collection of Mr. George H. Dalsheimer, Baltimore, Maryland.

Page 20. "Overhauling the Mariner's Friend," 1931. This image was generally printed as a carbro transfer photograph. A tedious procedure, the carbro process starts with a silver print, which is transferred onto carbon tissue and then onto a sheet of rag paper. The carbon image is physically raised on the surface of the paper; the highlights are thin and delicate, the shadows thick and rich.

Page 23. "Boys Swimming in the Patapsco River," 1933. This photograph appeared in the *Sun Magazine* in 1950 with an article highlighting 100 news photos that had been selected in a national competition from photographers representing 610 newspapers. The aim of the competition was to select images "depicting America's free children."

Page 24. "Roof Tops, Nuremberg," 1930. This photograph was made during the summer of 1930, when Aubrey Bodine, with no knowledge of foreign languages or any traveling experience, boarded a ship for Europe and spent three weeks touring France, Germany, and Austria. Bodine printed this image as a bromoil, a painterly technique produced by inking a bromide photograph with oil pigments.

Page 25. "Cambridge," 1929. This image is printed in reverse. One step in the carbro process requires transferring the exposed image from a silver paper to another surface. Unless the photographer has initially compensated for the technique, the image will print reversed. This is an early Bodine carbro, and he may as yet have been unfamiliar with this inherent characteristic. White chalk and graphite pencil have been added to accentuate the highlights and shadows. From the amount of reworking on the final print, one may assume that Bodine was satisfied with the structure of the composition, regardless of the reversal.

Page 26. "Gloucester Harbor," 1929. The original of this photograph is a blue carbro print.

Page 28. "Gloucester Dock," 1929. Similar to "Gloucester Harbor" (p. 26). A dated example of this photograph is printed in blue carbro. Gloucester is a small village located on the Ware River, east of Williamsburg, Virginia.

Page 29. "Chesapeake Bay Skipjack," 1933. A unique bromoil print of this image is in the collection of the Smithsonian Museum of Natural History. In *My Maryland,* Bodine identified this skipjack as the *Thomas Clyde.*

Page 30. "Conowingo Dam," 1936. This photograph was taken during the St. Patrick's Day Flood of 1936, when all the floodgates were opened to relieve enormous pressure on the dam. The Conowingo Dam is located north of Havre de Grace, Maryland, on the Susquehanna River.

Page 31. "Contour Plowing," 1937. Characteristic of Bodine's experimentation, this image (taken along York Road, outside Baltimore) was regularly printed in reverse and appears in *My Maryland* with the farmer and his horses moving to the right.

Page 32. "Main Sail, Doris Hamlin," 1939. Aubrey Bodine sailed the *Doris Hamlin* from Baltimore to Norfolk on assignment for the *Sun* in 1939. On its next voyage, en route to South America, the schooner was mysteriously lost at sea.

Page 44. "Emigrant Woman," 1939. A carbro print of this image was printed and dated 1939. This unique photograph was lent from the collection of Mr. and Mrs. Kent Minichiello, Washington, D.C.

Page 45. "H. L. Mencken," circa 1940. The only known print of this image is inscribed by A. Aubrey Bodine as a "kallitype"—an unusual technique developed in 1889. The kallitype process is similar to platinum printing, except that it requires the use of metallic silver rather than platinum chemicals. Printed with a tonal range and size similar to that of "Emigrant Woman," this Mencken portrait is also lent by Mr. and Mrs. Kent Minichiello, Washington, D.C.

Page 46. "Iced In, Spa Creek, Annapolis, Maryland," 1936. Bodine's caption in *My Maryland* indicates that this photograph was taken during a severe winter freeze in 1936. The boats are skipjacks, which have anchored in the creek for protection from the ice.

Page 48. "Oyster Tonger," 1948. This photograph appeared in a January 1949 *Sun Magazine* article that identified the setting as Tilghman Island, Maryland.

Page 53. "Choptank Oyster Dredgers," 1948. This photograph was taken while on assignment for the *Sun Magazine.* The large skipjack is the *Maggie Lee,* the small one on the horizon is the *Lucy Tyler.* Because of the stormy weather, Bodine had a difficult time photographing and was surprised to find this image when he developed the film. Not only did "Choptank Oyster Dredgers" win first prize in the 1949 Popular

Photography national contest, but it was also awarded medals in Canada, Sweden, South Africa, Hong Kong, France, the Philippines, Italy, Portugal, and all across the United States.

Page 54. "Skipjack Making a Lick," circa 1955. "Making a lick" is a waterman's phrase that refers to making a pass over the oyster rock while dredging under sail.

Page 55. "Sailmaker, Albert Brown," 1954. Bodine's caption in *Chesapeake Bay and Tidewater* identifies Albert Brown, from Wenona, Maryland, as the fourth generation of Browns working in a shop established by the family in 1870.

Page 56. "Chesapeake Bay Waterman," 1953. For a man who could not swim and never owned a bathing suit, Aubrey Bodine spent a remarkable amount of time on the water, photographing ships and the men who worked on them. His portraits, especially this one, indicate that he developed a friendly relationship with the watermen. This sailor is covered with water because Bodine had an assistant throw a bucket of water on the man just before clicking the shutter of his camera.

Page 57. "Melvin Collier, Deal Island Blacksmith," circa 1950. In *Chesapeake Bay and Tidewater,* Bodine says that Melvin Collier's hand-made dredges (one is seen leaning on the right of the photograph) were thought to have a "magic touch" and to produce more oysters than other dredges. Bodine always felt this blacksmith looked like the Duke of Windsor. When the Duke and Duchess visited Maryland, Bodine was assigned to photograph the couple for the newspaper. During the portrait session, he showed the Duke the blacksmith photo reproduced in his Bay book and pointed out the likeness. From all reports, the Duke was not amused.

Page 58. "Raking Clams," 1948. "Raking Clams" illustrated the August 28, 1948, *Sun Magazine* story with the subtitle, "A Large Group of Watermen on the Eastern Shore of Virginia Dig Clams with Their Feet."

Page 63. "Rowing at Ebb Tide," 1944. This photograph was taken near Havre de Grace, Maryland. Bodine did extensive retouching to the negative before he made his final exhibition print. A fine example of this photograph is in the Baltimore Museum of Art.

Page 65. "The Ward Brothers," circa 1950. Steve and Lem Ward were famous decoy carvers from Crisfield, Maryland.

Page 66. "Crab Dredging," circa 1955. Watermen dredge for crabs in the lower Chesapeake Bay during the winter, when the crabs have moved into the mud in deeper waters.

Page 67. "Deal Island Dead-rise Crab Skiff," circa 1955. Small workboats are often used on the Chesapeake Bay. This particular boat is native to Deal Island.

Page 68. "Fisherman, Loch Raven," 1950. This photograph appeared on the cover of the *Sun Magazine* in 1950 with an explanation that Baltimore's Loch Raven was opened to fishing in 1948.

Page 70. "The Gentle People," 1952. Bodine selected the title "Gentle People" for this portrait of young Amish girls made while covering a story on the Amish community in St. Mary's County, Maryland. The image won the National Press Photographers annual award for portraiture in 1953.

Page 72. "Bessemer Converter, Bethlehem Steel, Sparrows Point," 1946. Several variations of the scene were completed by Bodine. This particular image was printed on a rough textured paper, probably Gevaluxe, which allowed reworking the surface with white chalk as well as black charcoal.

Page 73. "Pennsylvania Train Yard, Baltimore," circa 1945. This photograph appeared in the *Sun Magazine* in June 1946 and again in August 1949. The smoke and sky areas have been heavily manipulated on the negative to reinforce the drama of the image.

Page 74. "Industrial Power," 1950. "Industrial Power" was the title Bodine gave to the photograph taken at the Bethlehem Steel Company Power Plant at Sparrows Point, Baltimore. This image won a 1951 medal from the Photographic Society of America.

Page 79. "H. L. Mencken," 1955. From their professional association at the *Baltimore Sun* and with their similar idiosyncrasies, Mencken and Bodine developed a strong friendship. This portrait was taken in Mencken's backyard on his seventy-fifth birthday. Bodine won a third prize of $100 from the Cigar Institute of America for this portrait.

Page 80. "Gathering Maple Sap," 1950. The photograph was taken near Grantsville in Garrett County, Maryland. In *My Maryland,* Bodine captioned this picture "Calling All Pancakes."

Page 84. "Baltimore Harbor, Night," 1949. Bodine's salon records list at least 96 exhibitions and countless medals for this image between 1949 and 1965.

Page 85. "Ship Chandler's Window," circa 1955. Bodine preferred to flop the negative of this image, thus enabling the viewer to read the window lettering easily. The Old Bay Line steamer *City of Norfolk* is visible through the window.

Page 87. "Longshoremen," 1955. These workmen were photographed on the B&O Railroad pier at Locust Point, Maryland. In 1960, this image was awarded a silver medal in an international contest sponsored by Rumania, selected from 2,875 prints submitted from forty countries. It also won a silver medal in Moscow (1960) and medals in Hungary (1959) and Yugoslavia (1961 and 1963).

Page 89. "Long Dock, Baltimore Harbor," 1947. Taken in the Baltimore Harbor, this photograph shows the steamer *City of Norfolk* on the left and the U.S.F. *Constellation* on the right.

Page 91. "Long Haul, Maine," 1952. Bodine enjoyed recounting how he made this photograph by paying the fishermen to get back in their boat so that he might capture the mood of the rainy day.

Page 94. "Tobacco Field," 1947. This photograph was used as an illustration in the *Sun Magazine* article "Tobacco to Burn," published November 30, 1947.

Page 95. "Checkers Game, Crisfield, Maryland," circa 1960. When Bodine submitted this image to a National Press Photographers Association contest he titled it "Next Move."

Page 97. "Beggar at Howard and Lexington Streets, Baltimore," 1968. This photograph was found in the files at the *Baltimore Sun* and was included in an article entitled "Men at Work."

KATHLEEN M. H. EWING has, since 1976, owned and directed a gallery in Washington, D.C., specializing in contemporary photography. She has worked extensively with the A. Aubrey Bodine photographic estate since 1979. Previously she held positions with the National Gallery of Art.

HAROLD A. WILLIAMS served in a variety of capacities with the *Baltimore Sun* from 1940 until his retirement as Sunday editor in 1982. He is author of a biography of A. Aubrey Bodine and is currently at work on a history of the *Sun*.

The Johns Hopkins University Press

A. AUBREY BODINE
Baltimore Pictorialist, 1906–1970

This book was composed in Meridien by Brushwood
Graphics Studio, from a design by Martha Farlow. It
was printed on 100-lb S. D. Warren's Lustro Dull
Cream by Collins Lithographing and Printing, Inc., and
bound in Joanna Kennett book cloth with Multicolor
Textured endpapers by Advantage Bookbinding, Inc.